DATE		

SPY WEDNESDAY'S KIND

SPY WEDNESDAY'S KIND

Francis Sullivan

The Smith  New York 1979

*distributed by Horizon Press (U.S.)
and McBride & Broadley (U.K.)*

Covers by Jim Kay

contents

IV   Terrible Poems

V   Exilic Psalms

I   POET'S LENT

Story Theater

Two hands
and a space of air.
Here are two wings
and a man wearing them.
He has nowhere to go.
Here is a lacquer box
to carry messages in,
and rice paper with this
message brushed on it:
If you die, I die.
If you live, I live.
He has no one to go to.
Here is a man
without wings
and a like woman
who desire the lacquer box.
This is the circle of pursuit
all three run.
The two have the lacquer box.
They sit by it and glow.
The man with wings
has no message.
Here are clouds he opens,
nothing said in them.
Here are the currents
of the sea saying nothing.
The cracks of the mountains
are not written on.
He is made of air.
He has no message.
Here is the path he takes

to them with the lacquer box.
He says let me see
the message
I had to carry.
They agree and open the box.
They smooth out the rice paper
on which it is written:
If you have, you live.
If you do not have, you die.
He snatches the box from them.
Here is the path
along which he escapes.
Here he runs into God
who has waited for the message.
When the box is opened
and the rice paper smoothed,
the two read:
If you love, you die.
If you do not love, you live.
God snatches the box
from him and he runs.
He is lightning the man
with wings chases.
Here is the smoking ground
where God hits,
where the man with wings
finds the lacquer box.
It is pitted with burns,
and God is not there.
He opens the box
and the rice paper says.
If you die, I die.
If you live, I live.
Here is the place he dies.
Here is where the box falls

with its message.
Here is the space of air,
and two hands
smoothing the air where
it happened.

Zen Narrative

A fierce Zen master
made tea of his eyelids
to stay awake to pray,
but he saw in the teacup
a bluebird scene
and wanted to taste
his own power.
So, he set out in the scene
a cat's paw branch,
licked his fingers and ran
the branch to stick snow to it.
Then he blew softly
on his soul to make crystals
to contrast with the grey fur
of the cat's paw sprout.
He snapped a bolt of blue silk
up over the branch,
rubbed it with quick strokes
to make heat lightning,
then trapped the light
in his hands and spread it
so there was space,
bright space, between the sky
and the branch.
Then he whistled.
And the bluebird spiraled
onto the branch
and was quiet
and cleaned its feathers.
But unexpectedly,
a thrush began to sing.

The master and bluebird
were stunned hearing it,
it was such joy.
The thrush lost all control
and every not all at once
worked the air up to a frenzy,
juices flowed, sap ran,
seed welled up in the master,
and the bluebird did fits
of flying under bridges,
through spare trees like a needle
of an elf sewing cloth.
There was no thrush to be seen
who rained its pure song.
The fierce master knew fear.
He expunged the cat's paw branch
from his soul,
and the bolt of daylight blue.
He drank the long tailed
bluebird from his cup.
But he could not stop the thrush.
So he put aside his power,
and he stopped praying,
and he slept long in the shade
of a rock, or, awake, let the sun
fall on him as it would,
and he said greetings to the women
and met their eyes even as they
hungered for each other.
And when the time was up,
he sat in the space
between two steep mountains
and watched the empty sky
they held, and the song stopped.
And his power returned.

So he rose up to speak to them
who watched him, and they heard
his voice as a thrush's voice
they could not see, and they
ran from him. He chased after
them for solace, but they escaped
down the mountains and left him
with his silence. It was pure joy.
He died from it. They could not
climb the mountains to bury
him because the thrush song
lived there. And some clouds.
So they taught their young
never to control beauty,
nor ever to be absorbed by it
or they would die as fiercely
in silence and alone.

Recounting a Tale

The man of suspicions
worked with white paper and ruler
to make his lines,
but tropical flowers seduced him
and spurts of songs
contraltos sang in pagan
and christian seasons.
So he was a man shaking
a terrible noise from his ears
and holding his hands up dangling
as he walked through bushes
back to paper and ruler.
A geometrized woman
came to him in a dream
one night and said
touch the rims of my breasts.
You will come back
always to where you start.
The nipple will remain
equidistant from its perimeter.
You will not ever doubt it.
Copulate with me!
The way in, the way out
is exact. My womb will be
elliptical. The child will have
logic and charm and sound
like the hum of spheres
in earphones tuned
to their retreating infinities.
He said yes in his dream
and he copulated with her
and woke up appeased.
But he began to cry,

against all truth.
He got up and moved
as if his room were filled
with tropical growth,
and he pruned, pruned,
looking for the straight vine
and purely circular orchid.
He fell down in a trance
where we found him
speaking from somewhere he was
we couldn't know,
but it was a place of wonder.
He said to himself,
and we overheard him:
The orchid is a line
you just bend;
its color is a shaken bow.
A woman is a line
you just straighten;
her song is a shiver you hold.
Your throat is a place
where thick leaves grow
and splash sunlight
in abandon on the ground.
Your loins are the sun
and the moon;
their child, a motion of the sea.
We sat him again
with his paper and ruler
because we did not know
how to bend or straighten
a line to make orchids
or a woman's song.
He was in a place of wonder.
His voice was filled with joy.
So we left him.

Further Instructions

A poet thinks within the whole,
he said, as within the red-giant star.
He may be a fiend.
You did not know this.
He may lay shells on garden walls,
blow them apart and make garbage
of tea roses. He may, he said.
Untruth is explosive. It works
in the spirit as shells.
When I imagined tea roses
as random beauty, careless forms
making of beauty a corner
of an eye, I knew for some poet
these roses were the way
to breach canals, or ring a town
with inescapable fire, there was
an image in someone's mind
of where to place death
as on a map of a garden of humans.
The image in the mind
is the poem. I have begun
to move with kin, he said,
those with an image in mind
and a virgin earth out there
staring wildly until she knows
what is coming, tea rose
or violation. The generals have visions.
Stranglers have visions. Their poems
are published. In my mind.
As if a fire blended with a fire.
When you know this, he said,
you are immortal, the page

of every poem, and time is not
a limit. The poems land in you.
They blend with your own.
There was a woman burning in
a tea rose who loved me,
to keep a flower, because behind her
came night with a cloth to smother
anything before it, and she was,
because she was her own night
with cloth in its hand for smothering.
So I ran from enslavement to her,
he said, and in the morning,
only frost rattled on the empty ground,
and she was gone and twigs were bare
and my spirit is dyed soft red
where she is now, he said. Soft red
where I want to scream
to the soldiery you have no right
to be false warmth, to open
the bodies of the flowers of people
with shells that are pretty
in their flash but leave the cold
of death burn the tricked petals
to a white-purple ash
any wind may scatter forever
irretrievably. When you are with
kin, you think within the whole,
he said. You are a poet.
Then you are immortal. You must
prepare for every poem.
They may be the poems of the fiend,
or hers of tea roses,
or yours, rattling frost mornings,
or a quiet cry, like hers,
against violation, or for an offering
of fire that sings on a garden wall
beauty for the corner of your eye.

Ars Amatoria

Resign first.
Then wear clothes that can't peg you.
They will be puzzled, not hostile.
Speak in complicated imagery:
war is a dust devil without a loin cloth on,
fascinated with his own erection.
Women dry their dead on rocks near him,
shirts they have beaten clean.
Seem to draw what you know from yourself,
as if from memory,
memory a witness put in you.
Seem to keep witnesses inside you
as if they were women you loved, or men
who had said things only to you,
how that evening was lavender silk pulled
over breathless faces,
over the lob of the mortar shells,
the heartbreak.
Be defenceless to feeling.
This will cause fear, to you, to them.
You will be fooled.
What you have will be taken away
unless there are gifts,
someone with a melody like scarves,
who wears them for you,
who talks about white azaleas shedding,
or crepe myrtles at hot noon.
Or someone who will put a word on the cause:
"This is holy, misguided;
it is the skin of the spirit which comes off,
so that flesh is fire and re-birth.

This heap is all reality gone stupid.
The stackers are black holes.
Speak next in simple imagery:
sweetpeas are demons if love is the sun.
Skulls are good ashtrays through the eyes.
The soul rips silently, burns silently.
The imagery must not remain distant from you:
I have more death in me than the dead
who do not know, and more life
than the living who are
pinball arcades busily ringing tilt.
You are then ready, and unpredictable:
the blades of grass are tote marks;
they are not crossed;
the final number has not been reached.
Someone's pencil will not cross,
not end the series.
Then events will come under scrutiny
on their own easels.
We will see everything that happened.
There will be models.
There will be language thick as smoke.
We will go out for air,
and our heads will buzz with questions.
We will experience everything
everyone experienced.
Someone's pencil will not cross
until we do.
Then someone will come wearing a scarf,
light blue shotting on white synthetic.
Then there will be a silence.
A love will begin to rise,
perhaps in everyone,
and no one will understand it,
as crepe myrtles do not understand the sun,

nor the skull why it grins,
nor the dust devil why it lies down
on the ground with orange flowers.
Then someone who has the pencil
that may end the series
places it within everyone's reach.
Then the wind begins
to tote up new blades of grass.

Conference. Not for the Record

You suffer this way when
you know, he said. Her body
is lovely. He creates beauty.
You respond in your body with a
jig and warmth. In your spirit,
it is otherwise. I have spent
days helpless, he said. The images
he and she caused came
however I went hidden to deny
them places to land. The wren
with the broken neck. Jesus
overturning turtle doves in the
Temple. Then pulling down the wall,
hurling rocks into the valley of
judgment. The saints running like
cowards out of their tombs toward
Babylon and respite. Magdalen
breaking off the glass toes of Jesus
one by one, muffling the sound
with her crying. Jesus walking
home on stumps. Magdalen behind
saying let me share your grief,
breaking off her glass hair and
laying it under his hobble saying
blessed be the feet of the Lord.
It doesn't matter to you
after a while, he said. Then
your suffering increases. He makes
beauty. She is lovely. Your body
jigs. You know they are killers.
You belong to them. They belong

to you. They look at you and
they go still but have ticks in
their faces. They look at you and
in their spirits shafts of light
from the sun are the knives
of anger they must undergo from you.
They are woman hills
set against a board and smiling
as each knife hits and draws
their shape to applause that lasts
as long as wind and leaves.
They are hills of terror.
You see it on their faces. You would
rip them out as phones.
When you reach that state,
you are a man of the spirit, he said.
When you know what they know.
Then she will be escaping
her own pursuit,
she after she, birds nose to tail
zigzag for one plot,
and he will be promoting trips,
cheap, to bleeding statues
overseas, for God's sake and
his livelihood.
You will be everyone.
Some of them will die from you,
and some will live.
You will spend your days knowing which.
You will know the difference
between God and man.
Your prayer will be perfect then.
And you will not.

Poet's Lent

When it happens now, he said,
I have a measure for it.
Murder is larger than I am.
I am not a circle
around the faces of the women
who have come for the body.
Football is smaller than I am.
It is loose change in my pocket.
I can fiddle with it,
and still tell you love is
larger than I am.
Someone loved the drummer
at the jazzfest more than I did.
I loved the banjoist, loved
abstracting the melody from
his noise, but the drummer
had only his rhythm to face
winning us and someone
loved him more than I did
and went with him into
everyone and came back saying
it would strip you down to
happiness to be in everyone's bones
and beating with the beat of them.
I am smaller than he is.
I am smaller than she is.
She is coming out of blindness.
She has pain from pure light
and she stretches over her own
body like a skin too sensitive
to cloth and to the rays of the sun.
She yearns for darkness where

she was without skin and light,
and there was no pain at all.
I am larger than a dog's tongue
asking if you love him.
I am smaller than compassion.
I am smaller than ignorance eating
ground food with its old gums.
I am smaller than obedience,
great passions of it scoured from
marble with a frenzied spoon,
the last tool in the studio left him
when the chisels have gone soft
and the old madman
has god almost finished and his heart
says ten strokes left.
I am larger than I am, he said.
I have heard the larks dive down
to catch their own song before
it hits the ground.
I am smaller than I am, he said,
I am puzzled by murder.
The grief of the women is too great.
Their faces are plums.
Their grief is too large for me.
I am too small, he said.
Oh, God! he said, I am too small.
Nothing fits in me
that is too large.
Everything fits in me
that is too small.
I am a banjoist, not a drummer.
I have never been in their bones.
I catch my song
before it hits the ground.
I listen to it.
It is too small for me!

II   INSIDE DOPE

Plights unto Troths

We are stripped
to where words begin
in each of us,
beyond the white mushrooms
in caves,
the roots buried by mulch,
beyond compost
whose rot speaks impromptu
and lifts our burden
to start words nowhere
in our bones,
or pubic regions,
or aftermaths of rottings,
but out of the no hat,
no rabbit,
no audience nothing of
before the glands
when with a snap I hold
a blue butterfly
in two fingers
and you a green hummingbird,
then quickly
a whistling hawk,
then you the white eyes
of cars leading the blind
around a smashup
in a dark rain,
then silence again
before glands,
then the coo of a wood dove,
the snap of an olive twig,

the chatter of a squirrel,
the cracking of walnuts,
then the silence,
the nothing,
the starts over and over,
I, I, am, am,
hungry, hungry space,
for you, for you, to happen!

The Plot

Brown sugar she
said to all tongue him,
"Tell me about St. John!"
"He," he said, "had itchy dreams
that rubbed on each other's skins
for the while of conflict
as bears every part on trees
with the roughest bark,
then fall fatigued
into hibernation,
soothed and triumphant"
"St. John," she said, "he!"
"He," he said,
"boiled his food
and landscapes in his sleep,
a storm with typhoon
in the womb of paints
coming, no child,
a horror gargling beauty
for its throat."
"St. John," she said, "no!"
"He," he said,
"had a breeze for joy
inside himself in the heat,
had the beads of a peach
on his lids the whole time
of the boil of the world
as its cook,
had tangerines for a wad
in his gums,
and over and over

like a mint
the taste of light,
as if his tongue blessed
him, and kept him sweet
boiling conflicts
of dragons with milky pregnant
maidens in the sky."
"St. John," she said.
He said, "Sugar," he said,
"I only make tea!"

Inside Dope on Fairy Tales

curly-tongue toad,
flick me from a tree
fat with the juices
I stole as a fly from pockets
of leaves hung out to dry!
eat a fly!
your eyes will round
their own corners
naked to the crotch
as dune buggy wheels
vroom, vroom,
down I go
and my buzz, buzz dampens
in you
where I have a silence,
and everyone thinks
I love it,
being a fly flicked
from a branch by a toad
and eaten,
but I was trying
to know how the leaves
mated in the daylight,
and gave birth only at night,
so I turned myself
into a robber fly
to watch,
and I found out about them,
and when you knew
I knew,
you ate me
to get all I know,
but I don't know anymore
how leaves mate.

Still Life

white and red
camellias
rot in a bowl,
as fruit,
but what they were
when ripe
and open
in clear water
cannot be annulled
even by their own
decay,
when they bend
too far back
and let go their hold
on their own pollen,
gold crumbs
stuck to small fingers
held up for
looks and licks
in the center of
a revelation of
what cannot be
annulled by rot,
if it has happened
once in a bowl
of clear water,
however soon
we put them in
the trash
to be a death
new camellias
cannot,
in their turn,
annul.

Lamentation. Cool one.

now that it has no beauty,
it is a tool, the body.
the air and the sea are not its infinities,
but its limits.
hang old crosses on it
carved from narwhal backbones.
they have no limits.
stale skin underneath the crosses will say it.
on a fresh breast
a cross gets brushed aside
as in a bazaar with clothes on the slave
when the front row wants to see her.
on a stale one
the thong and the cross are in relief
and the bidding is soft, persistent;
there is no time to the bidding,
you buy no time.
you do not buy the body.
the body is a tool.
it is within limits, it is a limit,
a beach for combers,
sound for the air to make when whipped
with switches.
it is as the peapod, the lima bean.
it is as the japanese lantern, as bulbs.
only another body
will come of it.
not an infinite sea, not infinite air.
another motion,
a thumb on the dottle in a pipe
or along the grain of wood,

or on the eye, the mouth, the breast
of the dead man's sinning senses
with fragrant oils of penitence.
then another unintelligible stop.
a stop. a useless tool.
and someone's hands spread.
it is so. the body is buried.
where it just is.
in limits. and the cross
falls through its breast and swings
in an empty space on its thong,
until it is dug up for treasure-trove.

Night Ship: For Her

Here, a black Haarlem tulip!
Here, a black velvet dress!
Here, an obsidian statue
of a rain god,
an onyx brooch for the dress,
a black tortoise-shell comb
to keep your hair up in back,
patent leather shoes,
a black chamois handbag,
a black leather volume,
a night sky all udder,
the darkest crew,
the darkest chantey in the
Deacon voice of Orthodoxy,
smoked glass for you!
Here, a black sun!
Here, a black moon!
Here, my pockets out
of ears, of tongue,
of hammerhead sharks' eyes,
my words in the pitch black,
snow, snow, pitch black
snow futilely on you,
yes, seed, male, futile
grain for you too,
corn for the birds your words
are, half-singing in dreams
on not a tree to be seen,
pinches of spice on
blood pudding rings
for the blind!

Here, the blind aboard!
Here, I am aboard,
I have no complaint!
I have the blackest I could find,
there is no light,
the warmest, the most beautiful,
the blackest I could find
from where they fell out of
people and out of life,
for your trip,
for your utter trip,
last, blind trip,
naked, fierce, empty-worded,
lax hair, lank loined,
eyes out, ears out, tongue out,
trip, senseless trip out,
mine, mine, mine!

A Self From One Object

a ping on a clear tulip glass,
or light caught in it,
the glow of visible music,
or it is a feeding crystal fledgling
of a crystal hummingbird
imagined over it beating stopped,
or it is pure waiting
made visible from abstraction
into a sturdy silence,
or it is emptiness,
and sterile and poignant,
in need of a liquid hands must
pour, or humid air
must sew on it bead by bead,
when it is not silence anymore,
but labor toward an unknown birth,
or is what one writes a love
on with a finger
and can then watch the love fade
as drops slide onto the name
of the beloved and efface it,
or it is the thought
that holds the form of a truth
and will not change itself
except for a violence
come to smash it, but apart
from a violence,
will keep its circular base
as if it kept a kiss to a cheek,
and its thin stem of a heron's
leg in a clear pond,
and its tulip bell.

Allegories,
For When You Fill With
Death

Forests for the young.
Seacliffs for the old
who watch birds' eggs,
pried loose, hit rocks
and make them goatees.
Until snow brings death.
Until fog brings illusion.
I love you up to then.
Afterwards, no feelings.
I stare as the arctic.
I chew as the sea does,
do not leave you alone
gravedigging, midwifing,
a track signal arm as
you change instantly.
It is my "eternal" state,
cold god at massacrees
naming every name down,
cumulus cloud knowing
every act and motivation
until its spatter of grief.
But I am grain sized
and scuttled by the wind.
Death is in the living.
Your eye falls and breaks.
I talk to the other one
It too slips and breaks.
Your face comes down its

pole and is folded right.
I talk to your backbone
the sun licks chocolate
from and leaves a stick.
Your sex drops a shoe
and we limp to a chair
where we sit and conclude
death is in the living,
the artifacts prove it.
We hear a baby sucking you
under your chamois shirt.
We pull off your shirt
and you have pebbles there.
You squeeze sap from trees
nearby and sugar its lips,
but it sucks again at you.
Afterwards, I conclude
living is off the dead.
Then I say both conclusions
to you, to your suckling,
as if I auctioneer them
both, going, going, gone,
as at a massacree
cold god accumulates to.
Until the breaking of snow.
Until the breaking of fog.

S28Y Phoenix-San Francisco

A dust storm was a woman-speck
in my eye, but a letting go loose
of everything out over all fixed
earth things I was, who, on that
flight into a dust storm woman-
speck in my eye, missed being
in her skirts blind, for at safe
heights, all her letting go loose
across miles was visible, un-
touchable, and only sand grains
on my teeth I was unable to
swallow or work free said what
way dust storms work into the
mouth, into the lungs, so that
whatever the height, she reached
teeth and lungs; it was reason to
take off quickly and climb, be-
cause she was brown earth forget-
ting her hand holds on open space,
forgetting tufts of grass, the lee
of boulders' soft flesh folds,
she was just go, and I was just
take, and the earth was go, skirts,
and hair, and I was on that flight.

Poolside

from altitudes
the sierras are knuckles
your body lying in the sun
with bones through
my body in the sun looking
feeling love
but turning away
to burn elsewhere itself
as a cleaner deed
like blowing seed from
a hand
on a summer desert
water-rippling
to its wind with its sand
a careful knowing
of you
blending with a blue
sky the palest
three quarters moon
or the white grains
of milk air
that grow whiter with
the sun's doings
and sun's watchings
the moisture
beads of the lotion
on your skin
over its sierra bones
leeches
that never leech
in their jars

put mouth to you as
the sun may not
if not low
and a going fruit
you bite

A Waking Dream

The woman
who blew out God
for him
is gone herself;
the man
who blew out night
for her
is gone himself.

These are my words.

They left none. They
hooded their canaries and
tore up their letters.

When she walked,
her calves played;
when he spoke,
he smelled of warm bread.

I must talk of their
emptied places;

a tea rose shakes in one
in a wind for me,
a belled cat watches
birds in the other.
A man and woman picnic.
Jets interrupt their talk,
and dogs and frisbees

and cops in a car.
Their emptied places cease.

These are my words.

God and night blew me out.

My place is filled with fire,
with fuel for it.

I must talk of them.

A man and woman are led in.

They are ignited,
and god is their flaming.

Love is what god's fire
is fueled with
by those who lead them in.

I remember when
it was not so;
her calves played,
he smelled of warm bread.

There Are Women, Or It's a Psalm

No to You!
You are white and cold fury.
But yes, blue and warm
veins on a breast.
No, black passion, You have
my fingerprints faceless.
Yes, You have small fruit, cumquats
in syrup, served me.
No, torch, I am the powder left
in the furnace, not a bone.
Yes, I am a wild, singing wire.
No to You!
Yes to You!
I am a royal thistle.
No, I will leap into the sea
when I am too much.
Yes, I will rustle all winter
without color.
I love fidelity in the dead!
No, You are grace.
Yes, You are pain.
I am charmed by the sound
when You form a word.
Its meaning flies like grackles.
Its sound, the bounce of a finch.
I am caught in Your mirror.
I am caught in Your face.
You make me love me.
You make me hate me.
No, You are a touch, a blessing
as a night breeze.

Yes, I will not say no!
No, I can't say yes!
I think there is death near.
I will not help it.
I will risk a skeleton's winter.
Yes, You are my tongue's.
Yes, You are my ear's.
I will leap into the sea
if I am too much.
No, You can hold me back.
If you sweep the odor of cut grass
across my face,
soothe a mocker's war song.
Yes, if You love me.
No, if You love me not.
No, if I kill You
if I love You not.
If I make You a blue fury,
or a grackle sound.

III   ORIGINALS/COPIES

City Poem 1

it is a purity,
her bare, deep brown back.
there is the cone, the cylinder, the ellipse,
muscles, blades, neck.
she is where the city begins
and moves outward, out of the express
you ride uptown,
     out to joy,
      to the well where it breathes fully.
the sounds that punch out patterns
on your spirit
     change to musical oil drum heads, soft melody
     from percussion, a large performer's grin,
     and sparrows of coins ringing onto a cloth.
the unconscious revelations appear.
those that strike notes.
the perfect lips of a diorite head of a Gudean,
the tar stroke eyebrows of a painter
pinched in examining gold clasps of Scythian nomads.
     the clatter of wheels
     on steel
     rises and puts a stride into a jazz piano,
     the left hand is a clatter that cleans
     and warms the love out of the heart.
lights are throws of cloth into your eye,
green cloth, red, yellow cloth.
they recede then into the inexpressive,
as she recedes.
her purity is an afterimage
carried more stops.
it is expunged upstairs by one bus leaving

the kerb, its blue exhaust fumes twisting
your face away.
>   but the blue of it is like morning
>   grand canyon blue, monoxide,
>   the blue of enamel,
>   though death,
the blue death of beef,
or oxygen starved lips.
it is the swelling snake of the heat storm
in from the mountains, miles high darkening.
it is a new purity,
as the whiteness of old skin, the red rims of old eyes,
parrots, but their complaints have beaks at you.
it is expunged,
the new purity.
it begins again in a downpour on the plaza,
whitened air veeing the ribs of a hall made of
giant matchstick lines parted by glass tubes
set as buffers and stays between them.
it is expunged
by a drab clearing.
there is left
an orphaned consciousness
looking in glass for glows,
in stone for the mother of rock,
in the air for dyes proper to silk,
in the motion of bodies for
the splash of grace from fountains
all day and night,
the dampened air pressing close onto the skin
the quiet chant back of grace to grace.

City Poem 2

broken bottle skyline,
no climbing this wall into an orchard of figs.
stay this side and deal in junk
as jackals eat up what lions leave,
cracking bones for their marrow.
love has new rubrics.
not faces to a crevice in a wall where an eye
and a soft voice have a body and promises,
faces between jackhammer sound
working up desire
and fruition in the looking at what flesh
may show in the instant before the next flesh
moves through the sound wall showing itself
as marrow for the eye.
love is a jackal outside the lions asleep
in the rubble of their kill.
pastels are in the sky,
the light red of not blood, the lace of not silk,
the flicks of not neon light,
then the stars of not street lights,
the flying shapes of not sharks cruising above
toward the orchard of figs
over the broken bottle wall.
love is an elliptical flame in a lens
stamping an almond shaped spot
on meat out of reach,
shopping
in stops, gos, waits, nos.
love is a search in trash containers
for red leather missing a buckle,
or bottle caps without portraits.

it is thumbing through photos of nudes.
it is walking by newsstands.
over the wall it is a windfall of figs.
it is speech through a crack with an eye.
no climbing this wall.
it is search for a silver llama pin,
for an earring with two snakes head-in mouth
out of a pierced ear,
for strings for acoustic guitars,
for hogshead cheese on dark bread with beer,
and talk of these things
leading to a meal of talk and a meal
of talkers with separate checks.
love is hunger on a full stomach.
it is the eye as jackal,
the eye gleaning trash,
at its distance from the trashers,
for the missing buckle.

City Poem 3

manhattan turns into states of flesh.

flesh is the plasm of feeling.

everything feels, greater or lesser,
everything else.
feeling runs in tremors, in motions
and in fixities,
from unconsciousness to consciousness,
truck to windowpane to teeth to him to
her cutting out for good, cutting in.

there is the single presence of flesh,
its myopia,
its hardening, softening, dereliction,
glow from the sun,
impassivity, passion and wilderness.
there is its body pinned to the ground
in dreams that wet it,
in dreams the tapestries of paradise.

flesh is without defense.
it has every key, it has every alarm,
it has police,
but it is found face down at dawn,
it is found in the park in the morning
going tree to tree
reading who was the lover who carved.

manhattan is turning into stone flesh.
it sings a mad song for its father
and its lover.

its lover keeps it from drowning in water.

"he killed my father.
he kissed the king his uncle on his ring
so we could be eternity
with daisies for our hair goodnight."

manhattan is the last drummer boy in his gums.

manhattan is the first princess in her training bra.

manhattan is the vigil of the saracens in rows.

manhattan is chastity, belt, lock, and key.

manhattan is the vigil of the templars in rows,

a holy war, a peace of god, a moratorium.

manhattan is barbarian, jewelled to her nose,

kissing the king, nose to ring, goodnight.

Rothko Chapel. Houston.

A hand rose, palm up,
from the desert
under the sun
and guzzled it. The vision
made us frantic.
We guzzled empty hands, cheated
of ecstasy, and are bald
in a nest together.
Someone photos the day as it dies
of the night as it is born, burns
the print to its dark colors, rust,
green, brown, separates them,
then paints our windows out.
Dread comes.
We are not here to see.
He is not there to see.
Dread.
Until the flies leave our tongues
and die on sills
or an old house where some light
gets through the bon ami.
Do not resolve this,
someone says.
This is ecstasy. Aphrodisiac.
Permits carnal knowledge.
And lies are mulch.
No one sees
no one is seen.
An egg is cracked into your palm.
Slurp its life.
No, I want an eye there,

someone says. Oxblood eye. Or
a jonquil's eye. A pearl's.
A nipple's, someone says. A baby's
on a cord uncut.
A sun pumping belly.
Someone says,
dry it to a steer skull profile.
Rake lines of dread in sand
around it,
so it's mother earth with you
always,
not seeing, not being seen.
When the hand rises
under the sun,
tilts it down a throat,
shudders and glories
in it,
there will be no dread,
no stir from us.

Holy Land: 1st Study

God is a member of the mountains.
God walks on torrent beds
white with drought.
God is a column of buzzards
over Massadah.
God is the uncertain place under
the glow of the lamps, the jumble of rocks,
along the Wall, in the full moon
that has no face.

There is no God.

There are some kisses
of the wind, of the desert.
There is some healing.
Someone has buried the dead.
Children beg coins
which corrupt them,
but they run and play.
Someone sees history returning
and puts his hand out
to stop it. His prayers stop.
His eyes swarm with everyone.

There is no vision.

It is poured from a bottle.
It smells baked,
or like barrels of spices.
It sings and throws leaves.
It sings and sprinkles water.
It sings and strangers sing.

Holy Land: 2nd Study: 1st Person

With the large, dark eyes of a woman
or a boy, the Wilderness
has come in to shop for dates and spices
in the bazaar that is hands.
I hear its babble about angels
who lay the dust or halt the sun,
its quarrel about demons who defecate
in the torrent beds, who live
in hyenas for their laugh and cunning.
I see someone fill a hand
with a ball of dates,
and the large, dark eyes of the Wilderness
are illuminated with a sweet taste.
I hear it talk of gold air
sucked in by the earth,
of the frenzied picks of the night watch
looking for the lost lodes,
and the weary clatter when the watch
troops west in the false dawn.
The cover of a barrel is raised.
I see a fluff of basil fill a hand,
and the large, dark eyes of the Wilderness
are softened by intense joy.
I hear it talk of the smell of water
walking invisibly along breakneck rims
at night, and of the sounds of hooves
following rock to rock,
and how prayers are of no use,
how you hear thuds of falling,
how the sweet smell walks by you
again, but something holds you down.

I see someone fill a hand
with garlic bread.
Then the voice of the Wilderness
wails out a psalm:
"God is stripped to empty hands,
to torrents without water.
Dates circle his hunger on buzzards wings,
and demons moist with whispers,
and night smells lure.
But angels clothe him with copper gold,
and the night sky gives him suck.
He quivers with the water of the sun
when it comes looking for the dead."
Then I hear the Wilderness eating
and snuffing basil.
Then I notice every hand has stopped.
The large, dark eyes are on me.
I put a coin in the hand of the Wilderness
as if it is a guilt.
Then I go with it back.
It smells of forbidden loaves.
It looks like nudists tanning.
It feels like the rubble marking graves.
I sit on a grave for a long time.
Then I love the blue sky and strength
of the sun and the fierce, brackish water.
I love the resistance of the rocks,
the cooling down of the night,
the hawk of the place.
Then I return and say to them
of the hands,
may you be blessed in your dates and spices.
They do not understand.

Holy Land: 3rd Study

Each God
will have your ear
in turn.
*
Love is he.
Here is his well and his moon,
shoulder and knowing wind.
Here you are,
strewn down a slope,
sheep and goats.
Love is select speech
to you,
for milking or eating you
later in the tents
of promise.
*
The land screams.
God rapes it out of eyeshot.
We will soon have
his children
to bring up without a father,
saying love is he.
Here is his beard
flowing from the mountains.
His eyes look up from
the waters
that wash your feet.
*
Saying,
here are his ginger anthills,
his linen mist

over the delicate colors
of orange trees,
the horns of his head
which are mounts of wisdom.
Here is the fat grass
of his pelvis.
Here is the cliff face
he promises from,
so many bees' mouths,
the trees he uses
to brush off crumbs.
*
Love is like him.
*
The impious have ears
like gouged rocks filled with rain.
The sun comes.
They are powder by noon.
*
The impious give you
leprous soap for your face.
*
We stop saying.
We stop loving his children.
*
We cannot stop.
*
The sunset is someone's rust.
The dawn is someone's saffron.
Someone's hawk is loose.
Shadow's are some printer's ink.
*
A place for clubfoot and beggar.
A place for bastard child.

*

The grass is cropped down to
the bread soil and millions are
coming for the bread soil
and they will die if not fed.
*

Someone's is the odor of cooking.

Church's Rome Again

I am not
beyond the nightmare
of pure spirit
eating up flesh, a piranha pond
of baptism.

Love is flesh.

I had hoped pure spirit
would be goldfish,
or tropical fish bewildering
in their variety.

My lyrics die on me
in a frothing water
which then, in time,
is glass blue with sky.

Aphrodite comes up,
a skeleton on a pole,
grinning into her robe,
to save Greek sailors.

She is draped on an azalea bush.
She is flowering bones and bees.
She is green, the old myth says.

Hummingbirds come
and build their nests in her.

What will I do
with my flesh?
It is just beyond ripeness.
There are ponds
splattered all over.

When I come out,
a skeleton on a pole,
I will save women sailors,
grinning at them
from a judas tree,
my purple thumbs up.

Marx, Jesus, Mao,
grin from your bushes,
save women and men.
Bankamericard,
Citibank,
save women and men,
sailors and hummingbirds.

Save me.

I love green throats
with ruby dots
preening above water,
and corded throats
singing anchors
out of dripping water.

But someone always
shoves the dream in.

Roma. Museo Delle Terme. 1976

Pagan marbles are holy.
Not the gods in them,
the men and women missing
heads or arms,
but with something still perfect,
half a head,
or an urgent torso
copied from a Greek original
lost in a siege.
Pray for their makers
who have nothing perfect left,
and their models.
Not for the gods in them
who reappear in Christian wood
or stained glass.
Pray for me.
I have something still perfect,
seed and loves,
and my catalogue naming
these marbles,
some dates, then silence,
so I can see
Apollo
is a young man's face
in shattered stone;
The Niobid,
a young woman, daughter, arrow
in her back;
Venus,
a perfect headless female
near a perfect, armless male.
Pray for us.
The news is coming in.

Something perfect is still
losing to a siege,
seed and loves, the names,
the models
from a Holy Land.
Pray for God
who has nothing perfect left,
who is it's maker.

IV   *TERRIBLE POEMS*

Terrible Poem

a prophet is
a plumb line hung from the dome
of a hawk's eye,

in on the murder
of shuttlecock pigeons,
in on the trumpets
of the four seasons
from the mumped corners
of calendar winds,

not outside the screech,
or the spin, or the flurry,

straight
when the leaves leap to death
not to stay behind broke,
when the thresher
lies to the wheat it strokes,
when frost
argues it is love's own drool
kept for a mush,

less than the clock
that marks every theft
with its second hand,
less than a thurible,
less than mine sweeps,

dumb
as drought,
as red azaleas
pinned to a green bush
and spayed of their tongues
by a chill,
as spit in the tubes of a horn,

when we
fall like lightning
on the last carrier flying back
and say
between bites of squab,
it was the sun,
it was useless wax gave,
it was overweening pride,
when feathers drop into view
like leaves that leap clear.

Orpheus with Guitar

It was said god took away his strings for his
transgressions, and he waved his hand over a
soundless hole as if it were a wing with no air
to beat. It was said he grew silent and had no
rancor, that he was left with plumages and scales
but no birds, no dragons, that the stays that
held up drapes of blue and green and mottle un-
tied and colors set on him with the teeth of
linen, the soft revenge of beauty as a love bite.
It was said he had visions laid on him, that he
was water with reflections, that he was the shad-
ow of rising mist, that he did not move because
he was where the birds and dragons were who had
gone, where the stays that draped the colors
were that had gone, and the linen of creation
biting him with only its blue frenzy, the green
its grating grass, and the leopard-sun muscular
trees crouched in their own limbs pawing him to
run to be trapped into running to stop to be
eaten not as the sun or trees eat not. It was
said he was still, beyond thought, beyond feel-
ing, but not cold or warm, only still. It was
said that was how he learned his transgressions,
when he felt the bites long after the biting,
when he was still and could not sing in his own
ear whatever he wished them to sing and could
not remember their screaming, if it was joy or
anguish, when he sang them what they would sing
in his own ear. it was said his strings were
given back. It was said he could not play songs
he could hear. His hand moved as a wing with

air the blue, the green, the mottled drapes of things, as weather moves things of blue and green and mottle. It was said he sat down with birds and dragons and they ate him. It was said they grew silent. It was said they found bites.

Vision with its Outcome

darkness the west
darkness the east
daylight between them

it is god against god

there will be debris

a man must choose
he is not a spray of
flowers nor of birdsong
nor the fall of dry twigs
in a rising wind

he is of god or nothing

his gods wear hoods
to the west to the east
they thicken themselves
there will be one god

the daylight will be
crushed like sugar cane
one god will pour out

white and red roses
will be pressed
one perfume will pour

men are now facing
toward their one god

each god inspects its own

men move east or west
into their god and two
gods press the daylight

the pulp of the roses
is falling for rain on
the faces that would not
look west or look east

the pulp of the daylight
dries into dust and goes

god east and god west
move in total silence
over emptied daylight

they strangle one another

they fall down together
and there is now one god
and no faces east or west

a man is no more nor
a spray of flowers nor
a birdsong nor a twig

there is only god around
only debris of god

Spy Wednesday's Kind

wartime

men have drowned
women have burned

not as autumn in color

all of them fall
into your spirit
with your autumn

not as enriching mulch

but as irony

they drown
as hearing in music
they burn
as loving in sacrifice

bodies in heat not
with maturing seed

all of them fall
into your spirit

near islands in rivers
out of reach
near gates of temples

the meltings of copper foil
beaten into false leaves
to replace the stopped seasons
where time does not live

still your spirit

its autumn
for them to wear down
who burn, who drown

to mulch, to seed

not as a fiction
not as a charm that
snuffs out fire

as you
your spirit, your autumn
as all
or nothing goes in it

For Holy Thursday

four words sit on branches
in the first green twilight
after the spring full moon,
plague, famine, war, death.
I hear each voice distinctly.

green moss,
fall for the squirrel
for a bed.
green leaves, make faces
for the children of the birds.
green sky,
insulate the lives of the garden
from the torches of heat,
the snap
and the falling of rotted wood.

I am with my words as
with a handful of leaves,
a wind in my hand eating
and no fear in its eyes.

the true passion of a man
is helplessness, his speech.

whoever spoke the four words
that sit on the branches was not
helpless, his speech was power,
the wings of his speech hideous.

green gravel, green water
hold for the last steps to cross you,
for dogs to catch their masters.
green clouds, keep breathing.
there are eyes following you
with their breaths
to have a last look at the first
green twilight.

no voice of ours brings on
a night or a morning.
no voice of our tunes light
so that everything is green.

the passion is in him who
makes it so and in him who
unmakes it with four words.

I hear each voice distinctly.

green words, sing for sleep
fresh as the air
of new growth the cardinal birds
nibble for easy food, their flame
tufts out of red, sing for sleep
the minute the two passions rise

and the four words flap in the trees.

Good Friday, a Recognition

when she killed herself, all metaphor ended. life
was not in likenesses; death was unlike anything.
I looked for living words, for the directest speech,
or for the silence of darkness, not for illusory
metaphor, whatever would engage my spirit outward
or inward from itself in a living line which, if
it broke, I broke, and whoever heard what I said
and believed it would break, would feel life being
taken away by meant lies. I do not have living
words. when I read surrealistic poems I understand
how metaphor avoids both life and death. when I
read pure description, I sense how much is kept
back by a wilful cutting out of all but scraps of
places. there was a time when talk of god was
exempt, but now I see that she killed talk of god
along with metaphor, because god is a likeness to
life and a likeness to death in the human. his
poignancy is our experience to infinity, as our
experience is his to particularity, especially our
innocence, and the charity we say is purified by
catastrophe. I know I am deeper in lies after
these words because they are metaphors despite
their dun dress and dull drum beat. this is what
her self killing does. it becomes the ruling
metaphor. it becomes the choker of flowers. it
becomes purple thorn bushes. it becomes the cru-
cifixion but tipped upside down by her on a va-
cant hillside with no hammers but the deeds of her
words done out. I do not have living words.
every time I speak now it is metaphor about life
and death. and she has killed them both.

Inspection. Holy Saturday.

This nest was poorly built.
It tilted when she landed in it.
You see the blue shells
just here, and traces of dried yolk.
Inside the trunk, the bees have
found a space, at this fissure.
The hive must be loaded.
But it will freeze in winter,
or it did. There is the line of ants.
A long time ago someone bolted those
upper branches together. I saw
a woodpecker hit the bolt straight
one day and he went through himself.
The tree is dead at the top.
The vine with yellow flowers
that's gone all the way up
shouldn't fool you. It's dead.
Though it's lovely, a flowering tree.
I saw an eagle hit a branch
with comfort in his eye.
It broke and the eagle fell
flapping down through the branches
unable to recover clear air
until it hit ground and jumped
clear, then limped in the air,
if you can believe it.
Hear is where we must put
the reflectors. Nail them here.
It's finished as a tree, but
has been a long time staying,
and it marks my mind.
Nail them right above the scars.

One car that hit it
had a boy and a girl in it and
she was naked. Some sheriff had
caught them at it and the boy
took off and didn't make the curve.
I have not ever been filled
with such pity. I walked around
this tree at odd times for weeks
and I nearly drowned in grief,
and yet I was detached because
I didn't know them.
I knew the tree and its guilty scars.
The other crash was less,
somewhat funny, as if a tea kettle
driven by a drunk hit it
and whistled and the driver got
out to argue with the other driver,
and I found them knot to jaw
blaming and blaming
while the car steamed its life out.
So, only twice the reflectors
have been knocked off.
But I've heard a lot of screeching.
When the tree goes finally,
I'll have to blow out the stump.
That's a treat. The dynamite takes
it up in a second. As if it
were a rag doll a child flings down
in a rage. The concussion
is a pure symbol of flattening.
Then I'll have to fill the hole in.
And put in grass. Which I
wouldn't give you two cents for.
Cars won't make that curve.
It will be dirt here after the tree
is gone. You don't remember dirt.

Easter Poem

This is awareness
that dies or never dies,
not a fish market appetite,
a nose for good chowder,
but watercolors of it in you,
if you sweat you wreck them,
the mystics' burning image
of the male or female god
reaching hungrily for love
and you mustn't budge,
as if it happens in between
watchers of a scarlet tanager,
their fingers in the right
page, unavailable knowledge
as the real one eats berries.
It dies or it never dies.
There is to be nothing in
the marshland where gold
stalks drilled all winter,
nothing where curses left
skid marks into the guardrail,
and he and she hated love
afterwards and mailed it back,
nothing where words came
burning with visions of
all souls tossing a laughing
phallus in a blanket.
It dies or it never dies,
steaming, motionless,
or never screeching love,
or never lust filled death,
or nothing, never!

Gospelers' Truth

you know the stories.
you turn audiences on with them.
you listen to yourself.
you hear nothing.

nor will anyone tell you.

spaces mean more,
between buildings, gaps on trains,
pauses, especially confused ones,
and mimes ready to begin.

not to deceive
becomes a hunger not to touch
food or drink or love
or counsel,
letting disintegrations happen
with integrity.

you see what goes on,
who creates life or destroys it.
the fictions are rush hour,
the faces all preoccupied,
the sensual patterns all worked out
with red and green lines
to tubes to follow.

you need a new story.
about the fate of spaces. how they
never protest, how they
return to life after trains pass,
or buildings, or deaths,
how they invite your sensuality
with a naked body,
minus rape,
minus jammed fingers.

the audience ignores you.
then you ignore yourself.

then you hire yourself out to tell
stories that turn them on:

skyline scenes with trains
raping them.

V EXILIC PSALMS

Psalm

I cannot justify myself to You.
Neither my good nor my evil
has found a right way to relate
to You in the peace of truth.

I want You to be a presence
forever, an attention like a clear
evening of unmarred cobalt blue,
clean of contrails and exhausts,

yet someone on whom good and evil
are written, not so punition later
is a swift, ordered task, but so
all that happens will stay living.

It is like a death to know a love
that stays living. Unexplainable.
An equal love can understand You.
But it is another death on the first.

For my evil, I offer images of granite,
porphyry, and jasper in three columns.
For my good, I offer images of rain
on stiff holly leaves and on pebbles.

For Your love, I offer images of bodies
in whichever moment they were fresh
before the mystery took away their lives
and we must dig trenches for them.

For the long time it will happen
to You, two songs, dirge and dance,
light from the hair of a running girl,
the hoarse shout of a boy with a fish.

Desert Psalm

this flower
is for your horizon
to give it a focus
and a fragrancy

there are your mesas
they have been fiercely made
the rubble of the making
is at the foot of each

it is all compassionate
as if long hair were cut
to allow the sun
to cure the head of mange

even fear of death
without water or shade
in this open
intensifies life
the colors of it, the shapes
their spikes and hammers

you are far from your wells
there is a pebble in your mouth

this flower is foolish
it has no fear
its birth and death
are watched

I sense your eyes on me

my life and death intensify

Psalm for a Mosaic

I will be illusory
to You
as the stones of Your black eyes
to me.

My hands in human hair are not so.
They are looking for black squares.

My love of the naked is not so.
Love looks for a soft stare back,
as of a night through clear glass,

my voice its breeze
cleaning each tessera of dust
so the color glistens.
It is a rainy night on paving stones,

or it is passion
and helplessness combined,
and I put them
in Your head for You
to look at me without blinking

as I stroke skin,
let voices fall on me,
fluff their images like pillows,
turn the color of their crime
with their crime,
the color of their blessing
with their blessing,

to have Your eyes
nowhere else
but fixed on my illusion.

Exilic Psalm

If I am naked, You are,
with voices only as means
to stop events, or urge them.

Chant with me:

"Harmony is trackless wheat,
long ocean swells.
The world is braided hair,
an apple face singing
alleluja,
grace comes as dew!"

It is too old.
Each image has become a weapon,
polished and aimed,
"Don't move!"

Move with me, dance
a dying swan, dying witch,
an Eloise, and Abelard
screaming on Pont Neuf
without his loins.

It happens to us.
We wake up the beast
with a kiss.

"Wheat in abundance
comes from greed.
Fight for the fish of the sea.
Tie women's tubes,
or men's. Then
grace will come as dew!"

Pray with me
for the threshed faces
for bins for them
other than our mouths
or the rat's mouth,
or the frog's.

Chant with me:
"Men are waves on gravel
rattling women's beads.

The wind is keen.

Women are waves on rocks
feeding men roars.

The wind is keen."

We are too old,
our images too old.

We chant for the weapons.

A Psalm or a Monologue

Touch the light.
It is gold and thin at noon,
like skin.
You must not hate it,
or I will too.
I am not strong about beauty.
If I argue for it,
it grows cold in my hands
like cup soup.

I have lost paint skies to someone.
I have lost a man's despair
over the bright earth
to someone with teeth newly out.
I said: "It is beautiful
when the bright earth will not
let you hate it and hope too."
He said: "Hope is not earthy.
It is clean and survives.
Michelangelo
beat at his last Pieta until
they stopped him,
but a nipple and a hand are ruined.
He had no hope in stone."

Touch the air
in the olive grove, it is silver-
green, the air of the wheatfields
dotted with black-eyed poppies,
it is lovely air,
or I will hate it too,

and lose it to You,
as words that fly into windows
and break their necks,
or as children in earthquake rubble
we find with our noses.

Here are petunias in a basket
sucking on black loam.
Their mouths are wet and loud.
They feel like skin.
They have perpetual motion.
They smell like a woman somewhere
in a room full of speech,
and they have their own light.

Psalm

Each bird that sits has a wish to sing,
but sings the same in each same tree.

Or it's be sassy and step on Your toe!
Or it's be brutal and bind You and gag You!

Or it's what? scattering lint to grow cotton
to bring You bales for Your justice balance.
Or what? rubbing their backs who have sores
to bring you collapsables opened for rain,
what? what? all wounds sing a-ring-around-a-rosy,
every car wreck is every mongoloid, every xerox,
trees are filaments every spring in a clear bulb,
every spring compresses air for a trolley ride!

What if You are two eggs broken in my hands
and I have no fire, no pot, to poach You in,
to keep You respectable eggs. I grin with the
others and hold You out like a wetting child.

But if ever a Buddha-face set with the sun,
it's You, and I know it. If ever a dark bear
hugged a medicine ball the way nighttime hugs
daytime and plays, it's You, and I know it.

If ever howls were heard and teeth heard biting
lead, if ever guitars stripped and danced with roses
in their cheeks and rain in the hearts of their heels,
and someone heard and stood up like a stoned bum,
it's You, You they sell here for teletype speech,
You they instruct as a fare box, You they sing to
on the same branches of the same every tree,
You the rags, You the jug, You the dancing drunk!

Lenten Psalm

In Memory of Thomas Michael Curran

I want You not to be
emptiness
or I will be emptiness
in love, in speech,
in recollection of then, of now,
and of tomorrow You prepare today
if You intend to be
emptiness,
and make of me the air
of midnight, of noon,
cleaned by light of dark shadow,
by darkness of light shadow,
pure air
on reddening charcoal,
on blue, on gray,
on whitening charcoal
gone by grains
unnoticed from its place,
its place
bare as a mouth
stopped from saying:
the love that was will be
if You are not to be
emptiness
and make of me
emptiness.

Each rock in relief,
each copper plum tree with
its nodes of fruit hiding

in the leaves,
the snarling saw that trims
the sycamore of its death,
the fireplugs,
the smooth railings,
every face hiding in the leaves
of its pleasure and pain
against the thief,

is in Your space,
and is Your harm,
or Your white rain,

or the mime will stop
and pick his teeth
and join the dance
for walnut meat,
and I will have no
love of You and be
a silence of my own
closed up in fruit
against the thief

in the leaves of a copper tree,

until I see
You have no space
with Your no power,
and I love this
of You,
who are the mime
in his own fruit
against the thief.

Psalm with an Air

I love this of You,
You have no power,
nor spectacle as the silversmith sun,
or the cat's eye half-lid moon
hungry for a bird star,
nor the worry bead rhythm of words
sat in the middle of lady ghosts
screeching walnuts from shells
with their barefoot dance,

the silence of You
in which all this moves,
space for a mime,
attention to his white ruff
and red cross eyes
as he shows how they rain
down on him,
the victims of the spells of power,
of love picking its teeth
with its finger stuck in its mouth,
and how he is stained with
them all over him
in red dots,
and You are the grief
and the yawn for breath
when it is too much to know him,
then silence again for him
to show how dogwood makes him sin
and shakes its blossoms down
in a white rain for a soothe.

Each rock in relief,
each copper plum tree with
its nodes of fruit hiding

Psalm. Mexico City.

You showed me Your good life.
You showed me Your bitter life.

You showed me my life alone.
You showed me my life with love.
You showed me my life with hatred.
You showed me my life with You.

They showed us unmarked graves.
They showed us carnal altars.
They showed us hummingbird suns.
They showed us our morning star.
They showed us our death's head.
They showed us our animal face.

We showed them six risen kings.
We showed them six glorious queens.
We showed them holy, pink flesh.

They showed us sweat turned glass.
They showed us prayerful floggings.
They showed us fasts and cries.

We showed them bleached cotton.
They showed us scream-red cloth.
We showed them precision watches.
They showed us corn leaf donkeys.

They showed us callous handgrabs.
They showed us elbows and teeth.
They showed us warm brown eyes.
They showed us mascaraed eyes.
They showed us appraisers' eyes.

We showed them stammer or silence.
We showed them watchers' eyes.

You showed me silence watching.
You showed me silence ripped off.
You showed me silence turned on.

You showed me Your good life.
You showed me Your bitter life.

Prayer

You may be right, divinity,
everything is nothing alongside You.
Love may be plucks on strings;
the hand, the mime of true music.

You will crush me, if so.

There are barer lands than mine,
without water.
The corn there is starveling.
The city, elsewhere than here, smacks
shells between two bricks,
as with meatless walnuts.

Some mornings are pregnant.

I want them with an earthly hunger.

Some are polished sea shells, nautilus,
or fragments of abalone. They plumb me
with an earthly joy I am lost in.

There are bare leaves elsewhere.
They have no memories of times together,
evenings in the smell of grapes,
or with carved wood of You splitting
at the cheekbones with age,
or in birth or death.

I want You with an earthly hunger.

Elsewhere, there are hungers greater.

Prayer

blue heron
of the tideland
stay
beyond my time and feed

any form, stay and feed

crickets,
friends who talk,
who do not know yet
love is sure
it loves

find it out

going
takes nothing away
with it

eyes,
sickle beak
of the heron, you
unlistening who speak,
have time to you
to feed
in the light
that is out with the sun

nudity
greater than water
or sound

touch everything

and go

Prayer Before an Icon

Our eyes are level.
You are in a passion,
on my scale,
of the instant life starts,
life stops. I am not.
I want several faces to
kiss to heat
they can carry off.
No secret to You in my eyes
they are there,
so spare You are,
as bone before scrimshaw.
I am spare now
seeing
You do not love someone else;
for You,
one face is born,
one face is dead,
by one, by one, by one.
I want You so,
because my kiss is secret
self, hot and good, but
half a mirror,
half a lense.
I love their faces and want them
spared,
as Your eyes,
but life and death not
passionless,
even if it means, like You, being
bone from time

spent, from love made, from
mercies dealt,
before the final carving in
of scenes.

Psalm

for Kathleen O'Hara

The bodies in the ground can plead
for themselves
as the misshapen who are born.

Everyone alive can plead with You,
every rock broken by cold or heat
or vegetation like pickaxes.

I'm watching for the axe to hit me.
I will see what plea I make.
Last time it was terror's.
This time it will be cool because
You are stuck to my skin like
frozen metal, You will putrefy with me.

The diet of the nostrils of God!
The eye filled of God! The spadework
and new grass under God's foot!

You may have this sympathy.
I know some wreckage. All human
wreckage is like it. Like convulsions.
As if all the color left the world.
My sympathy is small but right.

May the putrefying dead bless You
as You hold them. May the living
bless You as You hold their dead.
May I never forget You who do it.